The 5-Minute BIBLE STUDY MAP for Women

A Creative Journal

Print ISBN 979-8-89151-188-0

Published by Barbour Publishing, Inc., 1810 Barbour Drive, Uhrichsville, Ohio 44683, www.barbourbooks.com

Our mission is to inspire the world with the life-changing message of the Bible.

Printed in China.

Follow *the* Map *to* Know God *and* His Word More!

This fantastic Bible study journal provides an avenue for you to open the Bible regularly and dig in to a passage—even if you have only five minutes!

> **Minutes 1–2:** *Read* carefully the scripture passage for each day's Bible study.
>
> **Minute 3:** *Understand.* Read a brief devotional based on the day's scripture.
>
> **Minute 4:** *Apply.* Answer the questions designed to help you apply the verses from the Bible to your own life.
>
> **Minute 5:** *Pray.* A dedicated spot for prayer will allow you to talk to God about anything on your heart.

May *The 5-Minute Bible Study Map for Women* help you establish the discipline of studying God's Word. You will find that spending even five minutes focused on scripture and prayer has the power to make a huge difference. Soon you will want to make room for even more time in God's Word!

Date: ....

YOU ARE KNOWN AND UNDERSTOOD

Read Psalm 139

Understand

When God created you, He knew you. He didn't need an introduction and time to get to know your quirks and true self. From the moment His artist brush, sculptor hands, and creative mastery formed you, He knew you at the most intimate level. That fact is beautiful and frightening all at once.

On the other hand, we spend so much time creating and wearing masks—conforming to the people and situations around us in order to fit in, to be accepted, to feel normal—that it is a mystery whether we even know ourselves.

Start today by removing your mask. Come before your Creator and loving Father as your true self, the woman He created you to be. Lay your sins, your worries, your regrets, your requests, your heartbreak before Him. He knows you, and He *chooses* to love you, His cherished daughter.

Apply

Who (aside from God) knows you best?

Is it important to you that you feel understood? Why?

Pray

Date: ....

THE SHELTER OF THE MOST HIGH

Read Psalm 91

Understand

If you've ever had to run for cover during a rainstorm, you know that anything will do—an awning, a car, a shopping center, even a tent. Whatever serves to hold back the rain works just fine for you.

Shelters don't just keep out the rain; they provide a psychological covering as well. When you've got something over your head, you feel safer. That's how God wants you to feel when you run to Him with your troubles. When you hide under the shadow of His wings (as a baby chick would hide under its mother's wings), He's got you covered. He's like a papa bear, daring anyone to mess with His cub.

Here's an interesting fact: God wants to keep you covered at all times. But let's face it. . .we have a way of tucking ourselves under other, counterfeit shelters. Maybe it's time to do an assessment, to make sure you've got the right covering. Whatever you're facing, God wants to protect you as you go through it.

Apply

When have you needed God's protection and shelter? How did He take care of you?

How have you sheltered others under your wings?

Pray

Date: ....

YOU CANNOT LOSE GOD'S LOVE

Read Psalm 136

Understand

Psalm 136 repeats the phrase "His love endures forever" twenty-six times. It's as if the writer knew how easily we forget God's faithfulness, so after each statement, he reminded us (and himself), "His love endures forever."

The fact remains, if we are children of the God of heaven, we cannot lose His love. We are His forever—chosen, bought at a price, accepted, forgiven, redeemed, and a full heir to His kingdom.

Yet still we mess up, and doubt creeps in. We're not good enough. Not worthy of being forgiven for the same sin. . .again.

His love endures forever.

We worry and fret; anxious thoughts overtake us as we stumble through life. Forgetting that we've been saved and are protected by a mighty God, we try to fight our battles ourselves, sometimes pushing Him away.

His love endures forever.

You cannot lose His love, friend. Rest in that promise and thank Him for His steadfastness today.

....

....

....

....

....

Apply

How does the fact that you cannot lose God's love affect your relationship with Him?

How is God's love better than any other love?

Pray

Date: ....

ACCEPTING HELP

Read James 2

Understand

God loves you. All of you. Not just the spiritual parts. He cares about your physical needs as well. The body of Christ should always be about helping one another.

At times you will need help. You may feel tempted to say, "It's okay, thanks anyway, but I've got this." It may be hard for you to accept help. You may feel that you can do it all in your own strength. This may seem strong. It may feel brave. But, in actuality, what you are doing is denying others the opportunity to help you. This denies them a great blessing.

Remember how good it felt last time you extended a helping hand to someone in need? Be sure that you are also allowing God's people to bless you in your own time of need.

Apply

What is the difference between faith with and without works?

Why do you think James says that faith without works is dead?

Pray

Date: ....

HAVE YOU BEEN WITH JESUS?

Read Acts 4

Understand

Peter and John had been with Jesus. It was evident. They were warned not to speak of Him, but they said this was not possible. They knew Jesus, and they could not be quieted.

These were blue-collar fishermen called as disciples of Christ. And yet they boldly preached and healed in the name of Christ.

When people examine your life, do they know you are a Christian? Do you stand out as a Christ follower? Do you find ways to bring Jesus into everyday conversations? Or are you more like the teenager who wants her dad to drop her off a block from school so that no one will know she is associated with him?

Consider these things. Dwell on them. Pray about them. Make changes as needed. You want to be a woman who is known for having "been with Jesus."

Apply

Do others know that you have been with Jesus?

How do they know, or why are they unsure?

Pray

Date: ....

GOD HEARS YOU

Read 1 John 5:13–20

Understand

From an early age, children are taught that praying is thanking God and asking Him for things that they need or want to happen. If we're not careful, we can incorrectly think of God as a heavenly vending machine that will dole out the goods if we say the right words and push the right buttons.

But prayer is *not* about pushing our agenda and hoping God will be on board with it. Prayer is approaching our loving Father with a heart that sincerely wants to be in line with His. When we pray this way, the things we ask of Him will fit into His good and perfect will for our lives and His creation as a whole. And *that's* when He hears us and we will receive what we have asked for.

What is God's will? Ask Him to show you. Seek Him in His Word. Talk to friends who are strong in their faith, and see what God is doing in their lives. He's listening. He hears you.

....

....

....

....

....

....

....

....

Apply

Do you believe that God hears your prayers? Why or why not?

How can you know your prayers are in line with God's will?

Pray

Date: ....

POWERFUL PEP TALK

Read Joshua 1

Understand

God had called Joshua to be the one who would lead His people into the Promised Land after wandering in the desert for forty years under Moses' leadership. And in Joshua 1, you can read the powerful pep talk God gave to Joshua to help him be the brave new leader. It's not just for Joshua though. This scripture is a powerful pep talk from God to you as well, in whatever situation you find yourself. You have the whole Bible—the complete Word of God, including accounts of the life, teachings, death, and resurrection of Jesus Christ, plus the many books that came after the Gospels—to study, memorize, and meditate on. And you have the gift of the Holy Spirit living in you to instruct and guide you as well. So, just as God did for Joshua, let God lead you in the wonderful purposes He has for your life as you follow His Word with strength and confident courage.

....

....

....

....

....

....

....

....

Apply

How is God specifically calling you to be strong and courageous right now?

So far in your life, how has God given you success for your obedience to Him?

Pray

Date: ....

BUILT ON AND ROOTED IN JESUS

Read Matthew 7:24–27; Luke 6:47–49; Jeremiah 17:7–8; Colossians 2:6–10

Understand

If we're in the middle of a storm but have a solid structure to take refuge in, we still have a strong sense of peace. But if we're caught in a tent in the middle of an open field when tornadoes pop up or we're in a shack on the sandy beach of a raging sea, anxiety prevails. And we sure don't build a trustworthy tree house in a tree without strong roots. So, if it seems anxiety is prevailing too much in our lives, maybe we need to reevaluate and reinspect our shelters and foundations. Have we built on something solid that will last or on things that are weak and temporary? Are there any damages or cracks? Are we continuing to check and repair and strengthen our foundations if needed? Are we nourishing and growing strong roots? Everything of this world is shaky and fleeting, and only what is built strong on and rooted deeply in Jesus Christ and the truth of His Word will endure.

....

....

....

....

....

....

Apply

How do these four different scripture passages in today's study relate?

How can you strengthen your foundation and grow your roots deeper into Christ?

Pray

Date: ....

A PRAYER AND PROMISE

Read 1 Samuel 1

Understand

Hannah knew what it felt like to think maybe God had forgotten or didn't care about her. Can you relate? Maybe you too are desperately praying for children right now, and God has not answered that desire. Or maybe you've been asking God to answer other requests to no avail. Whatever the case, don't give up. Let Hannah's story inspire you and give you peace. She continued to pray for a son, and she showed her love and devotion to God by promising that if He agreed, she would let that son live at the temple to serve God his whole life. When God finally answered and blessed her with Samuel, Hannah followed through on her promise and was rewarded even more for her faithfulness.

And Samuel? He grew to be a great prophet for God. He was a blessing to all the people of Israel because of Hannah's faithful prayer and promise.

....

....

....

....

....

....

....

....

Apply

What prayer request have you prayed for the longest?

What do Hannah's actions say about her and her faith?

Pray

Date: ....

GOD'S REPLACEMENT POLICY

Read Acts 9:1–31

Understand

Saul was simply walking down the road, minding his own business, when God interrupted his life and brought lasting change. Maybe you've been there too. Maybe you lived your life your own way, according to your own terms, not caring what anyone else thought. Then God ripped the scales from your eyes and gave you brand-new vision to see things as He does. Amazing!

If you've ever experienced a radical transformation like that, then you can surely relate to Saul's journey. Out with the old, in with the new! God has a great replacement policy. He wants to take your old, broken life—the one riddled with worries, cares, and woes—and replace it with a new, whole one. He wants to point you in the right direction and win your heart. What an amazing and loving God He is.

Apply

Have you ever felt like you couldn't see clearly? How did you make it through?

If you've ever rebelled, what finally drew you back to God?

Pray

Date: ....

CHALLENGE YOURSELF

Read Philippians 3:7–21

Understand

If anyone should've been satisfied with the state of his faith, it was the apostle Paul. This giant of the early church experienced a miraculous conversion (Acts 9), after which he became a world missionary. He wrote nearly half of the New Testament and endured persecution and prosecution for the sake of sharing Jesus Christ. And yet, he knew he still had more growth to do, pressing himself closer to Jesus.

When you accepted Jesus into your life, it wasn't the end of the journey. Whether we've been a Christian for decades or are new to faith, each of us has space to advance toward our ultimate goal of eternal life with the Father, Son, and Holy Spirit in heaven.

What are you doing today to run the race? Sprinting, jogging, or walking, we're each at our own pace. Keep going and do not give up!

....

....

....

....

....

....

....

....

Apply

What are you willing to sacrifice in order to become more like Jesus Christ?

How can you push yourself in your faith to complete the race to heaven?

Pray

Date: ....

HE PICKS YOU UP

Read Psalm 40

Understand

Nobody—not even the most self-sufficient among us—can go through life alone. We each have our own struggles, temptations, pitfalls, and burdens that weigh us down and threaten to pull us into what Psalm 40:2 (NLT) calls a "pit of despair."

Because our Savior, Jesus Christ, stepped out of heaven and lived on earth, He experienced all these same issues. And He is faithful to lift us up out of any muddy pit of sin and shame we may find ourselves in.

There are any number of ways He rescues us. From the encouragement and intervention of a friend or a new sense of hope given to us by the Holy Spirit to a new perspective on a problem or a new purpose and peace that passes understanding—in a matter of a moment, the Father God can set you on solid ground.

If you're in a pit—no matter how deep it is—cry out to God. No hole is your ultimate destination. He will hear you and is faithful to answer. Soon you'll find yourself safely in His arms.

Apply

How has God lifted you up in the past?

Has God ever used another person to pick you up? How did you know?

Pray

Date: ....

A HARVEST OF RIGHTEOUSNESS AND PEACE

Read Hebrews 12

Understand

The word *discipline* doesn't always bring peaceful thoughts to mind. We might think of angry arguments and punishments of the growing-up years and other kinds of consequences during rebellious times in our lives. But Hebrews 12 shows us how we *can* view discipline with peace—by realizing the hardship we endure is the discipline from God that is good for us in a loving, fatherly way. If we let Him, He strengthens us and proves our faith this way—just like good parents shouldn't always rescue their children from every hard thing. Rather, they let them experience difficulty and consequences so that they can develop strength and confidence in their own capabilities, plus learn from their mistakes. Once we have grown up, we appreciate the discipline good parents gave us as we develop into mature adults who contribute well to the world around us. Likewise, once we have reached the other side of a particular hardship, we can see how God used it in our lives to develop us, plus produce "a harvest of righteousness and peace" (Hebrews 12:11 NIV) that contributes to His kingdom.

....

....

....

....

Apply

How has discipline produced a good harvest in your life?

What do you think it means that God is a consuming fire (Hebrews 12:29)?

Pray

Date: ....

TEMPTATION

Read Genesis 3

Satan appears as a serpent in Genesis 3. He tempts the first people, as he tempts believers today, in a sneaky manner.

Adam and Eve had heard God clearly. He had given them free rein in the garden. They could eat of any tree *except* one. He had not restricted them in a harsh way. They had great freedom. They were given one rule, one tree to avoid, one guideline to obey.

Satan was crafty in his approach, wasn't he? He uses this technique with believers today as well. Use caution if you begin to think to yourself: *Does God really have such a guideline for my life? Would He really limit me in this way? Is this really a sin? Is it really so bad?*

God's standards and His rules are for our good. He has drawn boundary lines for us in pleasant places (Psalm 16:6). Don't let Satan tempt you to believe otherwise.

....

....

....

....

....

....

....

....

Apply

Have you ever tried to rationalize a sin that you know you are committing against God?

What will you do the next time Satan tempts you to disobey God?

Pray

Date: ....

CHOOSE EXTRAORDINARY

Read Romans 12

Understand

Wake up; be awesome. Oh, if only it were that easy! But the messages the world shouts keep us feeling inadequate. We're not good enough, beautiful enough, smart enough, thin enough, or rich enough. Soon these messages take root in our hearts, and we're telling ourselves these same lies. Satan knows the ins and outs of that game.

But those lies don't have to be the words you focus on today. Choose to make this day extraordinary by living out God's plan for your life. Romans 12 gives guidance on how to do just that. Refuse to listen to the world's lies, and instead focus on the renewal that God promises. Focus on the talents God has given you, and use them—for His glory. Intentionally show God's love to those around you.

Your loving heavenly Father created you for more than a mediocre existence. Choose this day and every day to live an extraordinary life in Christ.

....

....

....

....

....

....

....

Apply

Who is one person you would describe as "extraordinary" and why?

How can you use your God-given talents to bring glory to God?

Pray

Date: ....

FREE IN CHRIST

Read John 8

Understand

Jesus' death on the cross paid the wages of our sin. He set us free when we placed our trust in Him to do so. There is no other way to be saved except through Him.

We are set free from the sins of our past, and we are set free from sin that easily entangles us. Living in a society that is filled with temptation to sin is not easy, but as a believer, you have the power to overcome temptation through Christ.

Thank your heavenly Father that you are no longer a slave to sin. Because of Jesus' death for you, you are completely free. You will never again be shackled by a lifestyle of sin, but instead, you will turn in repentance when you begin to take your eyes off Him and He will lead you back to His side. You are saved from sin, and yes, you are free indeed.

Apply

How is a sinner freed from sin?

What does it look like for you as a believer to be "free indeed" in today's world?

Pray

Date: ....

WHERE WILL YOU BE AT THE END OF TODAY?

Read Philippians 3:7–21

Understand

What's the state of your to-do list? Whether it's a mile long or blessedly under control, life is busy. Stay up late or get up early, we each have only twenty-four hours a day to get everything done.

There are tasks and responsibilities we must attend to, but the apostle Paul, writing to the Philippian church, challenged us to focus on the bigger picture—to make it our priority to know Jesus and experience the mighty power that raised Him from the dead.

How can you come closer to that goal today? If you're reading this in the morning, you're starting out the day right by spending time in His Word and in prayer. Lean on Him throughout the day too, and ask Him to guide your steps, your thoughts, your words, and your actions. Commit to seeking Him every day, taking a step (or a leap) closer to the glory of your brother, Jesus.

....

....

....

....

....

....

....

....

Apply

What can you realistically accomplish today?

Which goals are worthwhile pursuits and which aren't worth your time?

Pray

Date: ....

I NEED HUMILITY

Read James 4:6–10

Understand

There's a healthy kind of pride, a sense of God-given dignity that is the birthright of each of us—but that's not the sort of pride that this scripture is talking about. The word translated as "proud" was a Greek word that meant, literally, to think of oneself as better than others. *Humble*, on the other hand, meant someone willing to take a lower position. HELPS Word-Studies defines scriptural humility as "being God-reliant rather than self-reliant." When we rely on God rather than ourselves, we have humility.

Selfish, egotistical pride can form a hard shell around our hearts. Sometimes it takes the tears of genuine sorrow to wash it away. Then when we finally come into God's presence—naked, low, with no more pretense—He will lift us up.

....

....

....

....

....

....

....

....

....

Apply

How does pride act as a wall between you and God?

What feels good about pride? What aspects of pride have turned hurtful for you?

Pray

Date:..

YOU ARE RESILIENT

Read Zephaniah 3:14–20

Each day brings its own challenges, but life often hurls difficult seasons at us. For days, weeks, months, or years, challenging times can leave us weary and afraid, and may even threaten to defeat us.

What are you facing today?

Take courage, for you are a daughter of the mighty Lord. Be confident in the fact that you are a resilient woman of God—not because of your own strength but because God, the King and mighty warrior who saves, is with you. He will not make fun of you for struggling in times of distress—He wants to love you, protect you, and fight with you through it. He takes delight in you and rejoices over you with singing! He is your rescuer and the reason you can overcome any challenge you face.

Praise Him for past victories and stand strong in Him today.

Apply

What challenge are you facing today that has your hands hanging limp?

How does your perspective change when you realize that God is with you?

Pray

Date: ....

A CHEERFUL GIVER

Read 2 Corinthians 9

Understand

Have you read the picture book called *The Giving Tree* by Shel Silverstein? It's about a tree that gives and gives to a young boy. As the boy grows, his needs change. The tree willingly gives shade and its branches to the boy. The boy grows old, and the tree has become just a stump, having given tirelessly and completely. The tree meets his final need by providing a place for the old man to sit and rest awhile.

As the reader, it's tempting to grow angry with the boy. But in the end, we see that the tree was happy to give to the boy all his life. It found joy in giving.

Are you like the boy or the tree? Are you a taker? Or are you a giver? When you give, do you give with a joyful attitude? Or do you give so that you might be noticed or praised for your act?

....

....

....

....

....

....

....

....

....

Apply

When you give, do you do so cheerfully or begrudgingly?

Does your giving need any modification or fine-tuning after reading this passage?

Pray

Date: ....

POWERFUL PRAYER

Read Matthew 6:5–13; Luke 11:1–13; John 17

In times of stress when we just aren't sure how and what to pray, we can take a deep breath and go straight to the words of Jesus when He said, "This is how you should pray." Sometimes a bullet point list is helpful to follow when our minds feel scattered and unable to focus.

- Begin with praise to the Father.
- Ask for God's kingdom to come and His will to be done.
- Ask God to provide for daily needs without worry for needs of the future.
- Ask for forgiveness of sin and for help in extending forgiveness to others.
- Ask for protection from temptation and deliverance from evil.

We can apply the prayer that Jesus Himself instructed to every situation and need in our lives and in the lives of our loved ones.

....

....

....

....

....

Apply

What can you learn from how Jesus taught others to pray?

What can you learn from Jesus' prayers in John 17?

Pray

Date: ....

TAKE DELIGHT IN THE LORD

Read Psalm 37:1–9

Understand

Children are experts in delight. Watch a one-year-old gleefully play with the box her birthday present came wrapped in, and you are witnessing true joy. We can learn much from her today.

Our outlook determines how we interact with the world around us. When we're thankful for and take joy in simple pleasures, disappointments and frustrations become minor bumps in the day rather than catastrophes that derail us. When we count our blessings instead of focusing on what we don't have, we realize how well God provides for us. When we delight in the Lord and praise Him for His goodness and His perfect plan for us, we live safely in the center of His will—the very best place to be.

How is God delighting you today? Spend time looking for ways to be joyful. Whether He's doing big things in your life right now or you simply reflect on His unending faithfulness, live each day as an expert in delight.

....

....

....

....

....

....

....

Apply

What does taking delight in the Lord mean to you?

In what ways do you imagine the Lord delights in you?

Pray

Date: ....

TRUE REPENTANCE

Read Joel 2

How easy it is for us to stand in judgment of the Israelites as we read the stories of how quickly they forgot God's blessings. But we do the same, do we not?

When you sin, God is watching your reaction to that sin. He knows you will fall. We are living in a fallen world. But do you try to hide your sin? Do you diminish it, thinking to yourself, *Well, compared to this other person, I am not much of a sinner at all?*

Sin should break our hearts. God desires to see more than an outward expression of this brokenness. At the time of Joel, the people tore their clothing to express sorrow over sin. True repentance involves an inner sorrow, a tearing of the heart. God is quick to forgive when we come before Him broken and sorry for our sin.

Apply

What prompts you to be truly repentant of your sin?

How does God respond to your sorrow, regret, and repentance?

Pray

Date: ....

HE ANSWERED ME

Read Genesis 21:1–21

Understand

Abraham and Sarah were elderly when their son, Isaac, was born. No wonder Sarah laughed when she learned she was having a child. Not many women in their golden years give birth to babies!

Isaac was the long-awaited promise, the child they'd always longed for. His arrival was the culmination of many years of hoping, praying, and believing despite the odds.

Maybe you've been waiting a long time for something—a husband, a child, a new job, a home. You've pleaded with God, and it all seems to be in vain. You're nearly ready to give up. Circumstances have almost convinced you it's never going to happen.

Today, let your faith be invigorated again. Read through Abraham and Sarah's story and allow your heart to dream once more. God is a dream giver and a dream fulfiller. Allow Him to see this miracle all the way through.

....

....

....

....

....

....

....

....

Apply

Have you ever had to persevere like Abraham and Sarah? What happened?

Have you ever experienced a miracle in your own life?

Pray

Date: ....

YOU CAN CHOOSE JOY

Read Psalm 118

Understand

Psalm 118 starts and ends in the same way: "Give thanks to the LORD, for he is good! His faithful love endures forever" (verses 1, 29 NLT). This statement of praise and appreciation for God bookends a chapter filled with great challenges and great victories. Through hostility and attacks from enemies, the psalm writer continued to come back to the fact that God is the rescuer, that He hears and answers prayer, that He puts purpose and joy in each day.

What if you started and ended your day in joyful appreciation for what God is doing? "Thank You, Lord, for being so good to me. Your faithful love endures forever!" In the morning, set the stage for rejoicing in the day, and at night, before you lay your head on the pillow, thank Him again. Rejoice and be glad in today, knowing that God is working all things together for your good (Romans 8:28)!

....

....

....

....

....

....

....

....

Apply

Why do you think the psalmist still chose to praise God, despite difficulties?

How can you rejoice today even if you are going through a hard time?

Pray

Date: ....

HE IS ALWAYS KIND

Read Titus 3:3–8

Understand

Of all the characteristics of God, His kindness toward us is one that we should praise Him for every day. Kindness seems like such a simple thing, but it goes hand in hand with His passionate love for His children. His kindness allows us to approach Him when we know we've messed up. His care for us helps us to be confident that He will not condemn us in our sin when we sincerely repent and ask for forgiveness. His kindness was what resulted in His plan for our salvation through Jesus Christ.

We can't earn His kindness. He cannot be kinder to us or love us more if we say the right things or act a certain way. He loves us so much that He offers us new life in the Holy Spirit.

Your kind Father is waiting to hear from you. What is on your heart today that you'd like to tell Him? He will not judge you. He will respond in love. . .and in kindness.

Apply

How have you tried to earn God's favor?

Why is trying to earn God's favor a futile endeavor?

Pray

Date: ....

I'M PANICKED

Read Psalm 91

Understand

The original meaning of *panic*, dating back a few hundred years, had to do with the sort of contagious, unreasoning fear that can sweep through a herd of cattle—or a crowd of people—causing them to run into even worse danger. In fact, the original thing that triggers panic is often not even an actual danger; it might be merely a sudden loud sound or an event that startles us. Panic can be personal, but it can also sweep through an entire society, creating a state of fear that's so overpowering, we lose our ability to think clearly.

Panic is destructive—but we don't have to let it control our lives. Instead, as soon as we notice panic's poisonous touch, we can turn immediately to the only one who can hold us steady. God is our refuge, our place of safety. We can rest in His shadow.

....

....

....

....

....

....

....

....

....

Apply

How do you think panic is different from other kinds of fear?

How might scripture be the antidote for panic's poison?

Pray

Date: ....

WHILE WE WERE YET SINNERS

Read Romans 5

Understand

Christ died for us while we were yet sinners. In other words, He did not wait for us to straighten up and clean up and fess up and do better. We couldn't. We were incapable of living any other way until we met Him. We could not be "better enough" to come before a holy God. We were full of sin and we were in a heap of trouble. We needed salvation. And Jesus rescued us.

Remember this the next time you feel too guilty to talk to Jesus, too dirty to come into His presence, or too ashamed to pray. Jesus Christ went to the cross and took on all your sin. He bore the weight of the sin of the entire world. He carried His cross to Calvary. He willingly died while we were yet sinners. There was no other way. It was God's plan from the beginning to redeem His people from sin.

....

....

....

....

....

....

....

....

Apply

What state were you in when Christ died for you?

Why might you be tempted to clean up your act before talking to God?

Pray

Date: ....

MIND CONTROL

Read Romans 8:1–8

Understand

For most of us, our minds are in overdrive even before our feet hit the floor in the morning. Our brains are so jam-packed with schedules and responsibilities and to-do lists that we barely have time to think about anything outside of what must be done—now.

But even with an overloaded mind, there are still negative feelings or harsh criticisms or resentful feelings or spite or lustful fantasies that barge in. These thought patterns are all evidence that our sinful nature is in control, and Romans 8 tells us that it leads to death when left unchecked.

But that's not the end! Life and peace are there for each of us when we let the Holy Spirit control our minds. How? Right now, surrender your mind to God's perfect will. Ask for His guidance. And continue to give your mind over to the Spirit throughout the day. He is faithful to supply life-giving thoughts, grounded in the love of God.

....

....

....

....

....

....

....

Apply

How do you know your sinful nature is trying to control your thoughts?

How could your day be different if you allowed the Spirit full control?

Pray

Date: ....

LIVE IN THE LIGHT

Read 1 John 1–2

Understand

As Christians, we have found the light, but the world around us still dwells in darkness. Darkness comes in many forms, but it is always the opposite of God's best. God is light. He exposes darkness with light.

Those who are spiritually blind walk in darkness. They are on a sinful path. If they had the light, they would turn and take another path—the path that leads to heaven. But as it is, they are on the path to hell.

At times, you may feel as if you are in the dark. Depression may overtake you. You may feel that God has left you. He hasn't. It is at those times that you must rely on the truth of scripture. God has promised to never leave you. He has rescued you from sin and set you on a path of righteousness. Remember in the darkness what you know to be true in the light.

Apply

What is the opposite of light?

What do you think it means to live in the light versus to live in the darkness?

Pray

Date:

GOD IS IN YOUR CORNER

Read Hebrews 13:6–19

Understand

Confidence is such an attractive quality, isn't it? Whether it's someone who can easily command the attention of the room or speaks in public flawlessly or simply excels at their job, it's inspiring and motivating to see someone who has it all figured out. Spoiler alert: The truth is that most of the time, even confident people have real fears.

Real, lasting confidence isn't something that comes from within us and our abilities. And confidence that truly conquers fear is rooted in the fact that, as Christians, we have God on our side. He is fighting for us, protecting us, and making us strong in spirit, heart, and mind.

Where in your life do you need an extra dose of confidence? The Lord is your helper. All you need to do is ask for His guidance and His help. With Him in your corner, you can overcome anything!

Apply

Can trust in God and fear exist at the same time? Why or why not?

When anxiety starts to creep in, what can you do to remember that God is on your side?

Pray

Date: ....

YOU CAN BE CONTENT

Read Philippians 4:10–20

Understand

Contentment is one of those virtues that the world almost entirely dismisses. Why should anyone be content when there's always more to be had? More wealth, more power, more status, better toys, bigger houses, newer technology, latest trends. But all that striving leaves us exhausted, frustrated, and discontent in heart and mind.

So, what's the best way to practice contentment? Start with an attitude of thankfulness. When you take stock of the ways God provides for you, when you praise Him for all He's done, your heart will learn the secret to living satisfied and grateful in any situation. God will give you the strength and the untold peace that can be found only in Him.

Contentment doesn't come naturally to many of us, so start today by being intentional in thanking God. When you focus on His goodness, the world's shouted messages of "More, more, more!" will become nothing but background noise.

....

....

....

....

....

....

....

Apply

In what areas of your life are you most content? Why?

In what areas of your life are you most discontent? Why?

Pray

Date: ....

THE WATER'S EDGE

Read Psalm 23

He leads me beside still waters. How many times have you quoted those words? But have you ever paused to consider their meaning? When God leads us beside still waters, He's drawing us away from the cares and anxieties of life, far from the busyness, the harried schedule, the pressures of the day. At the water's edge, things are calm, still. The only things moving are the wind whispering through the trees and the gentle waters of the brook below.

He leads me beside still waters. . .so that I can rest my mind. Stop my crazy thoughts from tumbling through my brain. Quiet my heart.

He leads me beside still waters. . .so that my soul can be restored, my joy replenished, my hope resurrected.

He leads me beside still waters so that anxieties will cease.

Today, allow the Lord to take you by the hand and lead you beside still waters. You'll find all you need and more.

Apply

When has the Lord specifically instructed you to rest?

What's the hardest thing about resting for you?

Pray

Date: ....

GOD SEES THE HEART

Read 1 Samuel 16

Understand

Young man after young man paraded before Samuel. Their father, Jesse, probably watched Samuel expectantly. Don't you imagine he looked for a sparkle in Samuel's eye or a nod of his head to indicate the son who would be chosen to serve as king? And yet, Samuel said again and again, "This is not the one the Lord has chosen."

Jesse couldn't imagine that the chosen one could be the youngest, David, who was tending the sheep.

When young David stood before Samuel, the Lord pronounced him the chosen one. David was anointed with oil, and the Spirit of the Lord came upon him.

How do you see those around you? Or even yourself? Do you judge by the outward appearance or by the heart? God sees the heart.

....

....

....

....

....

....

....

....

....

Apply

What are some ways that we judge others?

According to 1 Samuel 16:7, how does the Lord judge a person?

Pray

Date: ....

A NEW YOU

Read 2 Corinthians 5:11–21

There's something thrilling about an extreme transformation. From a professional makeover to a weight loss in the triple digits, we cheer for the individuals in these stories as they seek to change themselves for the better. To gain more confidence. To get healthier. Their improved selves are revealed, and they often are empowered by the change.

These kinds of physical changes are well and good, but they aren't eternal. Only God can truly transform us into new creations, perfectly forgiven because of the sacrifice of Jesus on the cross. Our old, sinful selves *die*. We are no longer who or what we were, and God's great mystery of new creation happens. We're not a better version of ourselves; we are made *new*. And whole. And perfectly loved.

Have you grasped fully the fact that you are new, sister? You aren't used, washed up, or a secondhand treasure. Your new self is *here* now. Today, celebrate your newness in Christ!

Apply

In what ways do you try to change yourself for the better?

Why do stories about transformation resonate with us?

Pray

Date: ....

I DON'T KNOW WHAT TO PRAY

Read Romans 8:22–28

Understand

In childbirth, a woman moves past the ability to talk in coherent words. The process of delivery is so intense that every morsel of her being—mental, emotional, and physical—is completely focused on this amazing act that breaks her open in order to bring new life into the world.

In this passage of Paul's letter to the Romans, he compared our current state of reality to that intense process of birthing a baby. We cannot control our circumstances, any more than a woman can control childbirth. With that in mind, we don't *need* to know what to pray. After all, we can't tell God what needs to happen, and He doesn't need us to tell Him. Instead, we can simply surrender to the Spirit. God is with us in this process. He feels the same pain we do, and He will pray through us, birthing His Spirit into our hearts and the world around us.

....

....

....

....

....

....

....

....

Apply

Do you think it's important to pray eloquently? Why or why not?

When have you surrendered fully to the Spirit in prayer? How did it feel?

Pray

Date: ....

CONSOLATION

Read Jeremiah 31

Understand

Jeremiah is known as the weeping prophet. Maybe you can relate to that description. Perhaps you're the sort of person who feels things deeply, who has a hard time hiding your emotions.

The truth is Jeremiah had a lot to weep over. He faced persecution from those who disagreed with him, conflicts with false prophets, and untold plots against him.

Perhaps you've felt like that at times, like the whole world is conspiring against you. Maybe you've adopted a "What's the point?" attitude. Things are just too hard. The pressure is too great. Your anxieties have gotten the best of you.

If so, then look up! Your redemption is drawing near. Jeremiah's story ended triumphantly, with God's assurance that He would turn mourning into dancing. He will do the same in your life. No matter what you're going through right now, redemption is coming. God will rebuild, restore, and renew your life and give you purpose once more.

....

....

....

....

....

....

....

Apply

Have you ever felt inconsolable? How did you get through it?

How has God used you to console a friend or loved one?

Pray

Date: ....

I FEEL SO LOST!

Read Luke 15:4–7

Understand

In the Gospels, Jesus told three little stories that are all similar. In this story, a shepherd searches for a lost sheep. In another story, a woman searches her house for a lost coin until she finds it, and then she shares her joy with her friends. In the third story, a man's son runs away from home—and then comes home at last, where he is greeted with love and celebration. In each of these stories, where God is represented by a shepherd, a housewife, and a father, Jesus never implied that God blames the lost one for going astray. And He made it clear that the joy of being found is one that's shared throughout the entire kingdom of God.

When we feel lost, we can rest in the assurance that God is searching for us. He will find us, and when He does, even the angels will rejoice.

Apply

What makes you feel lost?

Do you think we are ever *really* lost to God?

Pray

Date: ....

A SOUND MIND

Read Luke 4:1–13

Understand

If you read the opening lines of this story, you'll learn a lot: Jesus was full of the Holy Spirit and led by the Holy Spirit into the wilderness. When you submit yourself to the Spirit of God, when you say, "I'll let You be the one to lead and guide me," then you're always in a safe place.

Like Jesus, we will go through seasons of temptation. The enemy will do everything in his power to veer us off in the wrong direction. We might even wonder why or how we got to a place of confusion.

But when we're full of the Spirit of God, when we're completely and wholly submitted to the process of learning all we can learn, we have to trust that God is still in control, even when we're in the middle of the wilderness.

Where are you today? Feeling a little lost? Wondering how you got here? Instead of questioning the Lord or letting anxieties get the best of you, ask the Spirit of God to fill you to the top. He will guide you exactly where you need to go.

Apply

Think of a time when the enemy came against you. Did you fall for his lies?

When you're tempted to give in to the enemy's tactics, what can you do to resist?

Pray

Date: ....

I'M EXHAUSTED

Read Isaiah 40:28–31

Understand

Life can be exhausting. Whether we're parents coping with the demands of young children, busy professionals with schedules crammed with meetings, or retired folk with to-do lists as long as our arms, we all sometimes feel as though we just don't have the energy to go on.

And yet we have to. Although we can take steps to simplify our lives, letting go of what's unnecessary, some tasks are unavoidable. Children and elderly parents need care. Our jobs have demands that are simply part of the work we've been hired to do. Meals need to be prepared, houses cleaned, lawns tended, and errands run. Life doesn't stop because we're tired!

Humans have experienced weariness since the beginning of time. And over the long centuries, God has promised us His strength. "Trust Me," He says. "Let Me do the heavy lifting. I am the source of all your energy. Let Me give you what you need to face your life today."

....

....

....

....

....

....

....

Apply

Do you ever feel guilty for being tired? Why or why not?

In what specific area do you need God's strength today?

Pray

Date: ....

GOD'S ECONOMY

Read Psalm 113–114

Understand

In this world, often those with power or money appear to end up on top. They drive the fancy cars, have the best jobs, and experience all the luxuries this life has to offer. In God's economy, things are quite different. He often chooses to exalt the humble.

God chose a prostitute named Rahab to provide protection for some of His men. He even sent His own Son to earth to be born in a manger and to be raised in the home of Joseph, a carpenter. Jesus called fishermen as His closest disciples, those who did life with Him throughout His earthly ministry!

Praise God today for being God. There is no other like Him, as Psalm 113 declares. Thank Him for seeing the hearts of men and women rather than just the exterior. Remember to see others as God sees them. They are precious in His sight regardless of their status or state.

Apply

How did Jesus humble Himself when He came to earth? Why did He do this?

When in the Bible did God choose the lowly over those with wealth or power?

Pray

Date: ....

THE BURNING BUSH

Read Exodus 3:1–17

Understand

When you're walking through a stressful season and you're looking for the perfect place to calm your nerves, the very safest (and most peaceful) place is the presence of God. When you cross over the invisible line into the holy of holies, everything else disappears. Worries cease. Cares flee. Troubles vanish. All the things that have kept your stomach in knots have to go in His presence.

What's troubling you today? Can you, like Moses, stand in front of the burning bush and let go of the things that have held you in their grasp? Can you toss them into His fiery presence and see them consumed? God longs for you to live in peace, and your first step toward finding peace is getting into God's presence.

What's holding you back? Take off those sandals and run into His holy presence today.

Apply

What does it feel like to be in the Lord's presence?

What do you imagine that Moses thought as God spoke to him from the burning bush?

Pray

Date: ....

LET THE LORD REFRESH YOU

Read John 4:1–26

Understand

Do you have plants in your home that are near death because no one remembers to water them? They start to look pretty sad, don't they? Or think of your lawn or garden in the middle of a hot summer with no rain. Sometimes we start to feel dry and ugly like that in our souls when we aren't spending good time with God. We need to read His Word and pray and worship Him so that He can lead and refresh us. We also need to fellowship with other believers who regularly do these things. God gives the kind of living water that makes us never feel thirsty again. When Jesus spoke to the woman at the well, He meant it for us too: "Whoever drinks the water I give them will never thirst. Indeed, the water I give them will become in them a spring of water welling up to eternal life" (John 4:14 NIV).

....

....

....

....

....

....

....

....

....

Apply

What makes your soul feel dry? How do you let God refresh you?

How do you apply verses 13–14 in your life?

Pray

Date: ....

GOD'S GOOD CREATION

Read Psalm 19:1–6

Understand

Our God delights in transformation. From the caterpillar changing to the butterfly to the seasonal cycles of the leaves of deciduous trees, creation constantly changes according to His masterful plan. The sky—what Psalm 19 refers to as "the heavens"—may be the best example of constant change. Consider how the sunrise's Creator uses different palettes of color and varying brushstrokes each day to fill the sky with beauty. And the night sky is no different as God directs the moon's phases and lights up the vast expanse with innumerable pieces of light.

The heavens say so much about God's greatness without using a single word.

Today, really look at God's creation. Raise your eyes to the sky. Kneel to be eye level with a child. Notice a flower or a bird's song or a dog's bark. He created our world—including you—for His pleasure and for our blessing.

....

....

....

....

....

....

....

Apply

When has God's creation awed you?

What does God's creation reveal to you about His character?

Pray

Date: ....

YOU ARE LOVED

Read Romans 8:1–39

Unconditionally—that is how God loves His children. These verses in Romans provide the Christian with a great deal of peace. Even death is not able to separate you from God's love. Why is this? You will not truly experience death. You have eternal life. To be absent in your current body is to be in the presence of the Lord. So even the moment that you take your final breath on this earth you will not be separated from God!

As you go about your day, remember that God's love surrounds you. He has declared you to be more than a conqueror through Jesus. In other words, in all things—trials, tests, hardships, and even your deepest loss or disappointment—you have the power to overcome.

You are an overcomer, and you are deeply loved. Claim the scripture and walk with your head held high as a daughter of the King.

Apply

What can separate the Christian from God's love?

What does it mean that you are more than a conqueror in all things through Christ?

Pray

Date: ....

MIXED MESSAGES

Read Genesis 11:1–9

Understand

Not long after Adam and Eve left the garden, an unusual event took place. The people (who had everything in common, including their language) began to build a tower to make a name for themselves. When God saw what they planned to accomplish, He chose to shake things up a bit. He confused their language and scattered the people.

Strange, right? God is usually all about unity, not division. Why split up the people? Why scatter them across the globe? The truth is these folks were getting a little too puffed up. They were looking at themselves as heroes, saviors. Yes, they were working together, but only to bring glory to themselves.

Maybe you've been in a similar situation where a team effort ended up being about personal glory. Or maybe you've seen excessive pride in a coworker or someone on a sports team. We can all get a little puffed up at times. As believers, we send a mixed message when we begin to tout ourselves instead of the Lord. It's time to refocus on Him, to take our eyes off ourselves so that He can be magnified.

....

....

....

....

....

Apply

When has a mixed message confused you?

How can you avoid the consequences that the people experienced in Genesis 11?

Pray

Date: ....

LIVE FOR TODAY

Read Genesis 19:15–26

Understand

Lot went through a *lot*. When it came time for him to leave Sodom and Gomorrah, God gave him specific instructions. He was not to look back. No gazing at the past. Unfortunately, his wife disobeyed God's commands and turned back for one last glance. She paid the ultimate price with her life.

Maybe you've been there. Maybe you've camped out in a place of unbelief and surrounded yourself with people who encouraged you to live the wrong way. You've done your time in Sodom and Gomorrah. But now you have regrets. You want out. God has a way of pulling you out of such places and seasons. When He does, you can count on Him to say, "Don't look back." "Don't let the past define you." "Live for today."

Take heart! There are better days ahead. Just keep looking forward and putting one foot in front of the other. And, whatever you do, don't be tempted to glance back over your shoulder.

....

....

....

....

....

....

....

Apply

When has God instructed you to move forward, but you felt tempted to glance back?

What's the most precarious situation God has delivered you from?

Pray

Date: ....

A FRESH START

Read Lamentations 3:22–33

Understand

Yesterday is done, and you messed it up again. You snapped at your family. You told that little fib at work. Through a lens of green, you saw the neighbors' new SUV and slammed the door of your junky vehicle a little harder than necessary. You told yourself you'll never be good enough, so why even try?

Yesterday felt like a train wreck, but today is a new day, and your Father God is here. He's saying, "Let's start again."

The truth is that God's forgiveness is available to us any hour of the day. He is faithful to show mercy whenever we ask Him for help. But time spent with our Father in the morning will result in a clear focus, renewed hope, and a greater understanding of our worth in Christ. It sets the day into motion in the best way possible.

....

....

....

....

....

....

....

....

....

Apply

What difference does it make that God's compassion doesn't run out?

Who in your life needs to receive daily mercy from you (whether they ask for it or not)?

Pray

Date: ....

I WISH SOMEONE UNDERSTOOD ME

Read Psalm 139:1–2

Understand

All of us have moments when we feel as though no one in the entire world understands us. It's a lonely feeling! We all need the sense that at least one other person understands our thoughts and feelings. That understanding would make us feel we're not strange or bad or unacceptable in some way. Without it, we feel as though there might be something wrong with us. We feel sad, rejected, alone.

In reality, if we had the courage to share our hearts with others, we'd probably find that they can understand more than we think they might. But until we have the confidence we need to reveal our true selves, we can allow God's understanding to heal our wounded hearts. Even if we think He is far away, even when we reject Him, He understands what we're going through. He is the friend who will never fail us. He's on our side.

....

....

....

....

....

....

....

Apply

Do you ever feel like others don't understand you?

How does it feel that God knows your most private thoughts?

Pray

Date: ....

ALL THINGS

Read Romans 8:18–30

Understand

Romans 8:28 ranks high on the list of verses that Christians commit to memory. You may have learned it as a song when you were a child or written it on an index card to remember the hope it carries: No matter what, God makes *all things* work together for the good of His children.

Not some things. Not just the easy things. Not just the good things. All things. The hard things. The heartbreaking things. The frustrating things. The moments when it seems like nothing good can come, God is working it for our good.

The unspoken part of Romans 8:28 is that we're often waiting while He is working. And waiting is hard. But waiting with the promise of this verse brings hope. What are you hoping for today? Ask God to reveal His work to you as you wait. He is faithful to deliver on His promises in His time.

Apply

How does Romans 8:28 give you hope?

What are you waiting hopefully for that you do not have now (Romans 8:24)?

Pray

Date: ....

CALLED TO HOLINESS

Read 1 Peter 2

Understand

A major way that Christians stand out in the world is by living good lives and doing good things. The choices you make regarding clothing, entertainment, and how you spend your money are noticed by those around you. People know that you are a Christian, and when you live a good life before them, you point them to Christ.

It's hard to argue with good results. When people see your children showing respect to others and making good choices, they will wonder what you are doing differently as a mother. When people notice that you support missions or give of your time to minister to others, they will wonder why.

One of the greatest ways to witness to those around you is by living a godly life before them. When others notice the difference in you, you can point them to Jesus. Our good deeds have one purpose—to bring glory to God.

....

....

....

....

....

....

....

Apply

Why should believers do good deeds? What is the purpose?

What are you doing to point others to Christ?

Pray

Date: ....

FAITHFUL FRIENDSHIP

Read Ruth 1

Understand

Every woman needs such a loyal woman in her life as Ruth was to Naomi. If you have that kind of faithful friend or relative, praise God for her and make sure she knows how grateful you are for her. Nurture that relationship. If you have more than one woman in your life like that, you are extremely blessed! And if you need a faithful friend, pray for God to help you make the connection. He knows and cares that you need good friendship, and He will help you find it. His Word says, "Two people are better off than one, for they can help each other succeed. If one person falls, the other can reach out and help. But someone who falls alone is in real trouble. Likewise, two people lying close together can keep each other warm. But how can one be warm alone? A person standing alone can be attacked and defeated, but two can stand back-to-back and conquer. Three are even better, for a triple-braided cord is not easily broken" (Ecclesiastes 4:9–12 NLT).

Apply

What motivated Ruth's fierce loyalty to Naomi instead of choosing to go with Orpah?

Have you ever felt as low as Naomi did? How did God lift you up?

Pray

Date: ....

IN THE MIDDLE OF EVERY STORM

Read Matthew 8:23–27; Mark 4:35–41; Luke 8:22–25

Understand

"Don't You care that we're going to drown?" the disciples asked. We feel that frustrating question too when we're in the middle of our own storms, right? We question how God can stay quiet—*Is He sleeping on the job?* we might wonder—and not intervene exactly when we think He needs to. *Don't You care about me, Jesus?* we desperately wonder and cry too. But when the disciples asked their question, it included a false statement. They were sure they were going to drown, and that was not true. Jesus knew they wouldn't. How often do we cry out to Jesus like He doesn't care, because we're positive we know what the awful outcome will be if He doesn't come to our rescue right away? But it's a false positive. When we stop, think, and humble ourselves, we remember that we surely don't know it all. Only God does. And He is perfect in all His thoughts and ways—which are far, far higher than ours (Psalm 145; Isaiah 55:8–9). Never forget that no matter what the storm is, Jesus will calm it, one way or another, in His perfect timing.

....

....

....

....

Apply

How do the accounts of Jesus calming the storm differ?

What storm do you need Jesus to calm right now in your life?

Pray

Date: ....

MANNA

Read Exodus 16

Understand

We often say, "Lord, I don't need much. Just give me what I need, not what I want." Likely, the Israelites prayed that too. "Lord, just a little food will suffice to see us through." Then manna fell like a feast from the sky. At first the Hebrew children were thrilled to have it. Then, after a while, it wasn't so tasty. They grew tired of it.

What an amazing story this would have been if the Israelites continued to praise and thank God for His provision instead of grumbling. If only they could have seen manna as a blessing instead of drudgery.

Maybe you can relate. What felt like a blessing in the beginning is now part of your everyday humdrum existence. You've forgotten to be thankful. The mortgage gets paid, and you don't remember to thank God. The electric bill is paid, and you let it pass by like it's nothing.

Every day God is blessing you. Don't forget to stop and thank Him for the manna!

....

....

....

....

....

....

....

Apply

When has God come through for you, pouring down unexpected manna?

How can you be a manna provider for others in need?

Pray

Date:..

HERE AM I. . .SEND ME

Read Isaiah 6:1–8

Understand

Isaiah found himself in an amazing position, didn't he? When the Lord asked the question "Whom shall I send, and who will go for us?" Isaiah was faced with a choice—to stay or to go. With no hesitation, he responded, "Here am I. Send me!" (Isaiah 6:8 NIV)

If you've ever spent time in God's presence, really drawing close to Him, perhaps you've had those little nudges. Maybe you've heard God whisper to your heart, "Go here," or "Do this" or "Do that." When the almighty author of the universe speaks, how do you respond? Ideally, like Isaiah!

If God reveals something to you during your quiet time with Him, don't be afraid. Simply raise your hand and say, "I'm here, Lord. I hear You, and I'm willing to go." But don't be surprised where He sends you once you've said it! Your journey is about to get really interesting!

....

....

....

....

....

....

....

....

Apply

When and how has God called you out of your comfort zone?

How did you respond to that call?

Pray

Date: ....

A TREK THROUGH THE DESERT

Read Joshua 1

Understand

The Israelites wandered in the desert for forty long years. A journey that should have taken them weeks took far longer. It was riddled with complications, rebellion, frustration, and so on.

Maybe you feel a bit like you're trekking through the desert right now. Your promised land isn't far off. You've got it in your sights. But there are times when you wonder if you'll ever pass over the river and actually enter. The process just seems too hard, the anxieties too great.

Maybe you're a couple of college courses away from your degree, but nothing is going right. Or perhaps your income is just a bit too low to get that house you're dreaming of. Maybe you're inches away from getting that job promotion you deserve and wondering if it will ever come through. You're right at the brink of your miracle, but it seems to be eluding you.

Don't give up! You will cross over the Jordan in God's time. And when you do, you can celebrate in style. Until then, don't continue to trek through the heat and sand. Stop and bask in God's promise. He will see you through.

....

....

....

....

Apply

When have you had to wait on a miracle?

What have you learned as you've trekked through the desert?

Pray

Date: ....

HE IS NEAR TO THE BROKENHEARTED

Read Psalm 34

Understand

God's Word doesn't promise a life of unbridled bliss for God's children. On the contrary, Jesus told us in John 16:33 (NLT), "Here on earth you will have many trials and sorrows."

But God is near, and during life's toughest situations, He will rescue us from despair. His path will guide us through and give us the strength to overcome anything. Maybe you've seen friends or family go through impossible things like this and come out the other side stronger in their faith.

Yes, God will walk with us, carrying us when necessary, through life's many trials and sorrows. But the best news of all is what Jesus said in John 16, right after telling us to expect difficult times. "But take heart," He said in the second half of verse 33 (NLT), "because I have overcome the world." Christ wins. We are victorious in Him.

Apply

Do you feel the presence of God more during times of joy or times of sorrow? Why?

When you've called out to God with a crushed spirit, how did He respond?

Pray

Date: ....

PERFECT HARMONY

Read Colossians 3:1–17

Understand

Our days can be full of conflicts—little ones and big ones, with family members or friends, coworkers or managers, strangers at the store or in traffic. On a really bad day, maybe you've had conflict with all of them. Sometimes we handle conflicts well, and sometimes we don't. As you reflect on your day, you might smile with satisfaction over how you controlled your tongue in one setting but cringe at how you overreacted in another. Or you might still be holding on to lots of anger and frustration. Whatever the case, give it to God, and remember that His grace covers you. Ask Him to reveal your sin and show you where you need to forgive and to seek forgiveness. Let Him help you communicate well. Don't run from all conflict or difficult conversations tomorrow, but as you face them, remember that you are one of God's chosen. You can demonstrate a compassionate heart, kindness, meekness, and patience. You can give grace and forgiveness to others because you know how much grace and forgiveness God gives to you. Let His love bind everything together, and let His peace rule in your heart.

....

....

....

....

....

Apply

What is an example of setting your mind on things above instead of things of earth?

What does it mean to do everything in the name of Jesus?

Pray

Date: ....

YOUR OWN WORST CRITIC

Read Psalm 55:16–22

Understand

Self-criticism is like a sharp sword that attacks our inner strength. It destroys the peace God wants us to experience. It can even make us believe that God has broken His promises to us. Self-criticism may seem like modesty or humility—but it's actually a demonic attack on all God has given us.

We need to treat those inner voices that tell us we're unworthy with the discipline they deserve. Sometimes, though, our strength is too weak to stand up to the whispers that slide like oil into our minds. When that happens, we need to turn immediately to God and call for help. He has the strength to carry us through this inner battle. His love will hold us firm.

....

....

....

....

....

....

....

....

....

....

Apply

In what ways do you criticize yourself?

What does God say about those things you are most self-critical about?

Pray

Date: ....

THE HEROES WHO HAVE GONE BEFORE US

Read Hebrews 11

Understand

Even the strongest Christian can get weary of keeping the faith. We wonder why God isn't answering a specific prayer or creating the breakthrough we think we need or proving Himself exactly like we want Him to. We sometimes have doubt and need to be honest about it. In those times, Hebrews 11 is such a powerful chapter to read to revitalize you. It defines what our faith is—being sure of what we hope for and certain of what we do not see—and gives us an incredible overview of so many heroes who've gone before us holding to their faith. This reminds us and inspires us to keep on believing and being obedient to God, like they did, even when we can't see all of His plans or the final result. If you are ever tempted to give up the faith, open your Bible to Hebrews 11. Read and reenergize. Think of how you'd like your name to be remembered among your family and friends and generations as one who never gave up on God. Though we cannot see all that He is doing right now, we absolutely will one day soon.

....

....

....

....

....

....

Apply

Which of the faith heroes described in Hebrews 11 do you relate to the most?

Do you feel like a foreigner and nomad here on earth? Why is that important?

Pray

Date: ....

FEAR GOD ABOVE MAN

Read Exodus 1

Understand

Shiphrah and Puah. They are not names mentioned at the average family's dinner table! Have you heard of them? As we read Exodus 1, we find that these two midwives are the heroines of the story! They were told to kill the Israelites' baby boys as soon as they were born. They feared God more than they feared the possibility of being caught disobeying the law of the land. They knew that God created and valued the life of each baby—Egyptian or Israelite. They had a holy reverence for life. After all, their job was to help women deliver their babies.

God does not want us to disobey the leaders of our government; however, there are times when this is the right choice. Pray that you would be as wise as Shiphrah and Puah to know the difference between times when you should submit to authority and times when you should not. As a believer, if something goes against God, you are not to do it even if your leader calls you to.

Apply

When is it right to disobey civil leaders?

What did God do for the two midwives of Exodus 1 because they feared Him?

Pray

Date: ....

REBORN!

Read John 3:1–21

Understand

Many Bible stories tell tales of men and women who messed up and wanted to start over. Thank goodness God is in the do-over business. He loves to offer second chances.

There's one do-over that outshines every other, and it's found in one little word: *salvation*. When we accept Jesus Christ as Lord and Savior, when we step into relationship with Him, we are reborn.

Think about that prefix "re-" for a moment. It means "again." When we accept Jesus, we're born. . .again. We get a do-over. A big one! Gone are the mistakes of the past. Washed away are our sins. Gone are the worries about who we used to be. In place of all these things, a clean slate. What an amazing gift from our Father God!

Apply

What do you remember about the day you gave your heart to the Lord?

When you explain salvation to others, how can you share your own journey?

Pray

Date: ....

I FEEL BETRAYED

Read Psalm 41:9–13

Understand

There are few things that hurt more in life than being betrayed by someone we love, whether it's a friend, family member, or spouse. Of course, all of us let each other down now and then; we're human and fallible. But betrayal goes deeper. It's a denial of the relationship we thought was so secure. It's like taking a step on what we took for granted was solid ground, only to find ourselves falling into a chasm. It may make us doubt ourselves and our own worth. The emotional anguish may make us sink into depression.

When the psalmist experienced this, he took his pain to God. Instead of begging his betrayer to change back into the person he thought he could count on, he asked God to be the one to restore his sense of balance and security. He affirmed God's love for himself and praised God.

....

....

....

....

....

....

....

....

Apply

Reread Psalm 41:12. How might you demonstrate integrity in your own situation?

When hurt and bitterness overcome you, can you make a conscious effort to turn to God?

Pray

Date: ....

YOU CAN LIVE WITHOUT FEAR

Read Isaiah 41:8–14

Understand

Fear is something like a strain of influenza. Just when we think we've figured out the proper vaccine to safeguard ourselves, the virus changes, and the flu rears its ugly head once again. And just when we think we've overcome our fear, some new worry or anxiety pops up, and anxious thoughts return, sometimes leaving us down for the count.

The only true cure for fear is unconditional trust in God. Faith that He will keep His promises that He's made all throughout scripture. He has chosen you. He will not throw you away. He is with you. He is your God who will strengthen you and help you. He will hold you up.

Do you believe Him? When your fears threaten to take over again, remember His faithfulness in keeping these promises in the past. He has never failed you yet, and He will not start now.

....

....

....

....

....

....

....

....

Apply

God will not throw you away. How does that fact make you feel?

How can knowing God is with you make you less fearful? Less discouraged?

Pray

Date: ....

WAITING WELL

Read Psalm 130–132

Understand

Many times in life we are called on to wait. We wait in lines at movie theaters and grocery stores. We wait for Christmas and birthdays. As humans, we certainly know about waiting. What kind of a waiter are you? Do you grumble or lose faith? Or do you patiently put your trust in God?

The psalmist said that his whole being waits for the Lord. When we rest before God with every part of our being, He meets us right there where we are. Seek to rest mentally, emotionally, physically, and spiritually before God. He is your Abba Father, your Daddy. He has your best interest at heart, and He is never early or late but always right on time.

Wait on the Lord, and claim the promises He has given you in His Word. He has not forgotten you. He will never leave you. He is your good shepherd. He will see you through, and the waiting will be worth it in the end.

....

....

....

....

....

....

....

Apply

Have you ever had to wait a long time for something? How did it feel?

What do you think it looks like to put your hope in God's Word as you wait?

Pray

Date: ....

GOD IS ALWAYS THE SAME

Read Psalm 102; Malachi 3:6; Hebrews 13:8; James 1:17

Understand

Life is always changing. Some of us thrive on that and some of us don't. We all have some things we love to change and other things we wish would always stay the same. No matter what changes we experience in our circumstances, relationships, and the world around us, it's so good to know that God is our one true constant. He is steady and strong and eternally true, and we can put all our faith in Him. We can build our lives on Him. We can trust that He is the perfect Creator with perfect plans and that He is sovereign over all places and times forever. That truth should fill us with a steady, strong peace that prevails throughout our lives.

Apply

What are good changes, and what do you wish would always stay the same?

How does it make you feel knowing that God is unchanging?

Pray

Date: ....

YOU DON'T HAVE TO UNDERSTAND EVERYTHING

Read Isaiah 55:6–13

Understand

If we can't be in control, it at least helps when we understand why something is happening. But God doesn't promise us understanding. In fact, there are some things about God we simply *cannot* grasp this side of heaven.

God says in scripture that His ways are "far beyond anything you could imagine" (Isaiah 55:8 NLT). That doesn't mean that He won't give us insight into what He's doing, but the fact remains that sometimes His plans may seem confusing and downright undecipherable to our human minds.

Rather than letting this scripture frustrate you, take comfort and encouragement in knowing that you don't have to understand everything. You don't have to have everything under control and figured out! God's ways are the *best* ways, and He will never leave you. He is working a perfect plan in you and around you.

....

....

....

....

....

....

....

Apply

How do you react when you don't understand the why of a hard time?

What does God promise during these times?

Pray

Date: ....

I CAN'T SLEEP

Read Proverbs 3:21–26

Understand

The Bible speaks of "wisdom" as though she were a person, making clear that wisdom is something far more than mere knowledge or intelligence. Some Bible scholars have even suggested that wisdom may be one of the roles Jesus took in the Old Testament. In any case, wisdom implies the deep sense of knowing that comes only from an intimate connection with God.

In this scripture passage, the author of the book of Proverbs advised us to actively pursue wisdom, to keep it constantly with us like a piece of jewelry we wear around our necks. This constant soul connection with God will make us come alive spiritually—and it is the best antidote for sleepless nights. It will allow us to relax, confident that God has everything under control.

Apply

What keeps you awake at night?

How does wisdom apply to insomnia, as this passage of scripture suggests?

Pray

Date: ....

THE VINE AND THE BRANCHES

Read John 15

Understand

Jesus described Himself as a vine and God the Father as the gardener. We are the branches. The fruits we grow on our branches are the good things we do for God that He has planned for us, the work He created us for—serving and giving to others, sharing God's love, and helping others to know Jesus as Savior.

We can't produce any good fruit unless we stay connected to Jesus, the vine. If you are feeling worn out and unproductive and like you're spinning your wheels at times, there might be an easy answer: You might need to check your connection to Jesus. Humbly ask the loving gardener to show you any problems and to nourish you back to nearness with Jesus. God can make you thrive again with lots of good fruit growing on you!

Apply

What good fruit are you producing in your life right now?

What ways can you improve on staying connected to Jesus, the vine?

Pray

Date: ....

SIMPLE ACTS OF KINDNESS

Read 2 Kings 4

Understand

The Shunammite woman saw a need and wanted to meet it. She recognized that Elisha was a holy man of God. She proposed to her husband that rather than just feeding Elisha a meal each time he passed their way, they should provide a room for him in their home. Isn't it kind how she planned the details? She decided that a table, chair, and lampstand in addition to the bed would go into the small room on the roof for Elisha.

This simple act of kindness and hospitality was not done for a reward. The woman did not ask for anything in return. But, amazingly, she was granted a son because of her gesture.

When you see a need that you are able to meet, meet it. The most basic act of kindness can make all the difference in someone's life. And God sees your good deeds. If not in this life, you will find your reward in heaven. The Lord is pleased when we serve and love one another.

....

....

....

....

....

....

....

Apply

When and how have you shown hospitality to someone?

Has someone ever been particularly kind to you? How did it make you feel?

Pray

Date: ....

THE GOOD SAMARITAN

Read Luke 10:25–37

Understand

Likely you've known this parable from childhood—the tale of the good Samaritan. Maybe you've skimmed over the story, convinced it has nothing to do with your current reality.

Then you pass by a coworker in her cubicle. She's crying because she's in an abusive marriage and doesn't know what to do. Or you drive by a man begging for food on the street corner. He's exhausted. Overheated. Completely defeated by life. Or maybe you receive a call from a friend riddled with anxiety because her child has wandered away from the Lord.

The truth is life gives us many opportunities to play the role of good Samaritan. Whether you're working at the church's food pantry, volunteering to coach at the neighborhood Little League, or letting a friend cry on your shoulder, you've got what it takes to minister to others. And God is very, very proud of the work you are doing.

....

....

....

....

....

....

....

Apply

Which character do you relate to most in this story?

Have you ever had a good Samaritan? How did this person help your situation?

Pray

Date: ....

IN SPITE OF EVERYTHING

Read Job 1

Understand

In spite of everything, Job did not sin or blame God. Let those words sink in for a moment. In spite of pain. Sickness. Death. Loss. Destruction.

Us? We're so quick to blame. When a meal isn't right, we blame the cook or waitress. When our team doesn't win, we blame the umpire or referee. When we show up late for an event, we're loaded with excuses for how others slowed us down.

Pointing the finger is a natural defense, but maybe it's time to adopt Job's attitude. Even when he lost everything, he didn't point the finger at God. He could have. (Let's face it, most of us would.) He could have pointed to heaven and shouted, "Why are You doing this to me? What did I ever do to You?"

The truth is, even in the hardest of times, God wants us to keep our eyes fixed on Him and our hope elevated. So toss those anxieties out the window. Stop blaming. Keep your eyes on the one who plans to deliver you; then watch as He works all things together for your good.

....

....

....

....

....

....

Apply

Have you ever blamed God for the bad things happening in your life?

Where is God when things are falling apart?

Pray

Date: ....

LOVE DIFFICULT PEOPLE

Read Luke 6:27–35

Understand

Most of us are conflict avoiders. Apart from those rare few who are wired to enjoy a good combative exchange, we intentionally structure our lives to be harmonious in whatever ways we can.

But there's always that person who is just so difficult. Maybe it's a coworker who seems to sabotage your efforts. Maybe it's an in-law who has never warmed to your presence in the family. Maybe it's someone who struggles socially, and it comes across as disrespect, creating awkward situations. Maybe it's simply someone who doesn't like you, and they make no qualms about it.

Jesus says love them anyway. Do good to them. Respect them and pray for them. This might be one of Jesus' most challenging commands, yet He demonstrated it over and over in His ministry on earth. With His help, you can do it.

....

....

....

....

....

....

....

....

....

Apply

Who is the most difficult person in your life, and what makes them such a challenge?

How could your perspective change if you make it a priority to pray for this person?

Pray

Date: ....

GIVING

Read Malachi 3

Understand

What is the first money you spend after payday? Whether it's the beginning of each month or at the end of each two weeks, you probably have a regular day that you receive payment for your work. One of the greatest habits a Christian can form is that of giving back to the Lord. After all, everything we have comes from Him in the first place!

First Corinthians 16:2 points out that believers should give regularly, individually, and in proportion with our income. Many believers give 10 percent. Others start with this and increase their giving. The exact amount that you give to the Lord is personal, between you and God. What matters is that you give not out of duty but cheerfully (2 Corinthians 9:6–7). The Bible promises that those who give generously are, in turn, blessed. This is a promise you can take to the bank!

Apply

What is God's promise here in relation to tithing?

Do these verses motivate you to give regularly to the Lord? Why or why not?

Pray

Date: ....

CONFIDENCE IN GOD

Read 1 Samuel 17

Understand

As a shepherd, David was to watch over the sheep. This job entailed fighting off wild animals that intended to kill the sheep. David had become skilled at his work. God had protected him. He had not died from a bear or lion attack, and for a shepherd, these were very real possibilities.

What David had faced in his past enabled him to face a new challenge with confidence. But notice this: It was not David's confidence in himself or in his own strength or ability that led him to fight the giant. It was his trust in the Lord.

"The Lord who delivered me" was the one David bragged on, not himself.

Look back in your life. Where has God protected or delivered you? God will use each of your experiences to prepare you for the next. Be prepared for a greater challenge that lies ahead.

....

....

....

....

....

....

....

....

Apply

What gave David the confidence to fight Goliath?

What gives you confidence to face an unknown future with a known God?

Pray

Date: ....

THERE'S MORE THAN THIS

Read Revelation 21:1–8

Understand

This old earth is broken and full of sadness. Stresses pile up and frustrations mount. Loss leaves us reeling, and pain is inevitable. In seasons when it feels like Murphy's Law reigns, we begin to wonder if the hurting will ever stop.

Revelation 21:4 is an encouraging Bible promise that we can cling to during the darkest times. Eternity for Christians includes a new heaven, a new earth, and a new reality that we simply cannot comprehend. No tears. No death or mourning or crying or pain.

Even better—God will make His home with us. He will dwell among us, closer than a next-door neighbor. We will have unbridled access to Him and all His goodness and mercy and love and abundance.

No one can say for certain what heaven will be like, but imagine what amazing things lie in store. And praise God for them.

....

....

....

....

....

....

....

....

Apply

How does knowing there is something more after this life help you face today?

What is one way you imagine heaven might be like?

Pray

Date: ....

YOU ARE CONFIDENT IN HOPE

Read Ephesians 1:15–23

Understand

Where light shines brightly, you can be confident in your next step. You don't fear unseen obstacles or holes to fall into. You can see your surroundings as they are and not wonder what's really out there. That kind of bright light was what Paul was praying illuminated the hearts of the believers in Ephesus—light that leads to greater understanding, spiritual wisdom, and confident hope in today, tomorrow, and forever.

The hope we have through God's grace is not a mystical, vague feeling that everything will be okay. Our confident hope is a complete, steadfast understanding that we will be victorious through God. This certainty comes to us through the Holy Spirit, who works in us.

Just as the sun rises each morning, ask God to flood your heart with His light. He will give you confident hope as you face today's challenges. You've got this because God's got this.

....

....

....

....

....

....

....

Apply

How does knowing that God calls you His child give you confident hope?

What does it mean that you are God's rich and glorious inheritance?

Pray

Date: ....

EVEN THOUGH THE SHIP WILL GO DOWN

Read Acts 27:18–28:2

Understand

Paul was a prisoner on a ship in a horrible storm, and his words to the crew and other passengers were somewhat comforting but very unsettling too. We might wonder, *Why didn't God just stop the storm? Why let them shipwreck at all?* But we must remember that God has never promised to always protect us from shipwrecks—literal or figurative. Yet even in the midst of them, He can save our earthly lives. And what He does promise is heavenly life forever when we trust in Jesus as our one and only Savior.

Just as God promised, eventually Paul and everyone on board the ship were safe. And we see how God provided for their needs through the good people of the island they landed on. This account helps give us peace when we feel our own ships are going down. Even when they do, God will always provide the people and resources we need to survive and then lead us on a new course according to His will.

....

....

....

....

....

....

Apply

Have you experienced a life shipwreck? How did you see God rescue and provide?

How have you experienced God's peace after a big failure?

Pray

Date: ....

GOOD FRUIT

Read Galatians 5:13–26

Understand

Have you ever wondered why the various fruits of the Spirit are called "fruit" in the first place? Perhaps it's because a fruit is something sweet that is produced when the vine is healthy. If you have a healthy orange tree, you'll yield a healthy crop of oranges. If your grapevine is robust, there will be juicy grapes attached.

The same is true in your life. If you stay close to your Creator, rooted and grounded in Him, your spiritual life will be healthy and robust. You'll begin to produce fruit for all to enjoy—love, joy, peace, forbearance, kindness, goodness, faithfulness, gentleness, and self-control. You won't have to summon these up; they will come as a natural result of spending time with your Savior.

So prepare yourself for a fruity future! Brace yourself for days filled with love for others, joy even in the midst of sorrow, unexplainable peace even when things are going wrong, patience with even the most annoying customer at work, and gentleness with your kiddos. God can do all this and more when you stick close to Him.

....

....

....

....

....

....

Apply

Are there any fruits lacking in your life? How can you remedy that?

When you're anxious or upset, which fruits are most beneficial to you, and why?

Pray

Date: ....

CHOOSE TO BE FREE

Read John 8:31–47

Understand

Under Old Testament law, there existed a way to be right with God, but even the most righteous could not follow every rule. The way to freedom was shackled with unachievable requirements.

Without Jesus, sin had a death grip on each of us. Our own selfish desires and destructive habits and thought patterns kept us oppressed, fearful, and clinging to our own filth because, we thought, at least it was *our* filth, and we were comfortable in it, even if that meant we were a slave to it.

But that false sense of comfort was and still is a lie from Satan, and the life-giving truth of Jesus is the only way to break free of the death grip of sin. "Now a slave has no permanent place in the family, but a son belongs to it forever," Jesus said in John 8:35 (NIV). Because of what Jesus did, you are a beloved child of God, dear to Him and an important part of His family.

Today, Jesus has set you free. Grasp on to the truth of your worth, your value, the preciousness of your salvation, and be free!

Apply

Where does the world say we can find freedom? How are these flawed?

What is keeping you from experiencing the complete freedom that Jesus offers?

Pray

Date: ....

YOUR FATHER SEES

Read Matthew 6

Understand

Have you ever received an anonymous gift? Perhaps it was something small like a candy bar you found on your desk or in your mailbox at the office with no note attached. Maybe it was a larger gift such as a debt that was paid off by an unknown hero. How did it make you feel?

God wants His children to give generously. His favorite type of giver is a cheerful one (2 Corinthians 9:7). And He sees when we go about giving in a quiet manner. God doesn't want us to get the glory for our gift. Instead, through our quiet or anonymous giving, He receives the glory!

Give God all the glory today. Perform a random act of kindness and smile as you walk away, knowing that you are not looking for man's praise but a reward that comes only from your Father in heaven.

Apply

What are some charitable deeds that you have done, or thought about doing?

Why do you think God wants believers to do these deeds in secret?

Pray

Date: ....

DAILY PURITY

Read 1 John 1:5–10

Understand

We Christians talk a lot about forgiveness and rightfully so. God's forgiveness and grace are essential to our faith and salvation. But God's forgiveness is a bigger concept than simply pardoning our sin. The forgiveness available to us through the blood of Jesus Christ purifies us just as if we had never sinned in the first place, leaving us holy, righteous, and blameless in the sight of God.

God's perfect forgiveness offers us purity. It makes us without blemish and whole. Because of that, we can stand confident before the King of kings and Lord of lords. These are the things we gain when we humble ourselves and confess our sins to God. Confession leads to transformation as we grow to be more like Christ. There's no other way to start again, to join Him in the light of His goodness.

Start the day in confession. Admit where you've failed. God is listening, and He will purify you again.

....

....

....

....

....

....

....

Apply

Why is it important that God offers us forgiveness time and time again?

How does forgiveness feel on a heart level?

Pray

Date: ....

THE NAME OF THE LORD

Read Exodus 20:1–21

Understand

It has become common in our culture to misuse the name of God. "Oh my. . ." followed by the Lord's name is a phrase that rolls off the tongues of even young children. Why? Because they hear it everywhere. The phrase is sprinkled into every movie and TV show. It is an exclamation spoken by adults all around them, often even their parents and teachers. And so they assume it must be okay. But is it?

God gave Moses ten commandments for the people to follow. This was God's law. One of the Ten Commandments states clearly that we are not to take the Lord's name in vain.

Are you taking this command seriously? Are you honoring the name of your God? Do you use it when you are speaking to Him or sharing with others about His great glory? Or do you use it as a slang word, defaming your God each time it is spoken?

....

....

....

....

....

....

....

....

Apply

Do you take the Lord's name in vain? Why or why not?

Are there ways to use the Lord's name in vain without actually speaking His name?

Pray

Date: ....

YOU DO YOU

Read 1 Corinthians 12

Understand

Too often, we compare ourselves to others and wish we could be like them. If you find yourself doing that, let 1 Corinthians 12 refresh you. You have been given the specific gifts, talents, and personality you have on purpose by God through His Holy Spirit. He has plans and purposes that are unique for you. You are not supposed to be exactly like anyone else because God wants you to do you. By incredible design, God will work what His plans are for you in coordination with what His plans are for others to create unity, love, and care among believers. When the church does this as God intends, it is the best way to display the great love He has for us and help others want to become believers as well.

Apply

How has God shown you what your gifts, talents, and abilities are?

How are you using your gifts to serve God and others?

Pray

Date: ....

THE GREATEST OF THESE IS LOVE

Read 1 Corinthians 13

Understand

Perhaps there is no chapter in the Bible quoted more often than the Love Chapter. You hear 1 Corinthians 13 most often at weddings. Love is the greatest of all the gifts. We read that, nod, and say, "Sure. I get it." But do we?

If love supersedes all, then we have to share it, even when we don't feel like it. When the neighbor's dog digs a hole under the fence. . .again. When the woman in the parking lot rams into your car. When the clerk at the supermarket double charges you for something but doesn't want to make it right.

Love has to show up in every relationship, every encounter, every disagreement, every bump in the road. When you offer it to others, you're truly offering them the greatest gift.

Is love leading the way in your life today?

....

....

....

....

....

....

....

....

Apply

Why does God consider love to be the greatest, most important, attribute?

When God says that faith, hope, and love continue forever, what does He mean?

Pray

Date: ....

GOD KNOWS YOUR NAME

Read Isaiah 43:1–13

Understand

As small children, we instinctually give names to the possessions and people dearest to us. From a name for a beloved toy or a pet to a loving nickname for a sibling or a grandparent, putting our own label on something seems to say, "I've claimed you. You are mine."

God does the same for us, His cherished children. He doesn't merely group us all together and love us as a mass of humanity. No, our Father God calls us *each* by name. He promises to be with *each* of us when we are going through difficulties. He has ransomed *each* of us and claimed *each* of us as His prized possession.

Our Creator knew us before He formed us. Before our parents imagined our names, He knew us and claimed us. Listen for His voice as He whispers your name today, and know that your identity is in Him.

....

....

....

....

....

....

....

....

....

Apply

How does God demonstrate to you that you are precious to Him?

Whom can you encourage today by reminding them that God knows their name?

Pray